THE CATFISH
INTERVIEW

The Catfish Interview:
Five Questions to Ask if You Want to be Happy at Your Next Job.

Copyright © 2022 by Jon Corteen and Jon Rotter

All rights reserved. No part of this publication may be reproduced, distributed, or transmitted in any form or by any means, including photocopying, recording, or other electronic or mechanical methods, without the prior written permission of the publisher, except in the case of brief quotations embodied in critical reviews and certain other noncommercial uses permitted by copyright law. For permission requests, write to the publisher, addressed "Attention: Permissions Coordinator," at the address below.

Printed in the United States of America
First Printing, 2022
ISBN: 979-8-9850546-3-7

Summit Press Publishers
411 Walnut Street #12515
Green Cover Springs, FL 32043-3443
author@summit-success.com

Quantity sales. Special discounts are available on quantity purchases by corporations, associations, and others.

For details, contact author@summit-success.com

THE CATFISH
INTERVIEW

Five Questions to Ask if You Want to be Happy at Your Next Job

By Jon Corteen and Jon Rotter

SUMMIT PRESS

Table of Contents

Introduction 7
One Big Happy Family: Question #1 21
Know Thy Self: Question #2 29
Good One Moment, Iffy The Next: Question #3 37
A Big Bag of Carrots: Question #4 45
Bye-Bye, Warm and Fuzzies: Question #5 55
Conclusion 63
Author Bios 71
Attention Leadership! 73

Introduction

You're looking for a new job. Maybe you even have a bunch of interviews set up. But a lot is riding on this move, on your final choice, so you're feeling a little nervous.

After all, you know how easy it is to wind up in the wrong place, despite the great pay and benefits. You know how easy it is to expect one experience based on what you've been promised, only to discover anything but.

Maybe you wouldn't call your current work environment toxic, but you can see how one might say that. *Wish I would've dug a little deeper on the front end of this job*, you think, *because I've got myself a disaster.*

Sure, you may be more jaded than a recent grad who has yet to be burned, but you share that deeply held belief that no amount of money is worth despising your job. Grind forever and retire old is not your motto.

You're not down for the Sunday night blues, feeling trapped, having to tolerate guff to keep some job. Those seven days a week are way too precious; you don't want to waste five of them for a paycheck. Those days need to fuel your sense of meaning and purpose—why else were you put on this planet? Money is good, but being happy at work is far more important.

So, here you are, preparing yourself for the interview process.

You know how to present yourself in such a way as to get a job offer; that's no longer the fear. It's that you've analyzed opportunities before and gotten it wrong thanks to one missed red flag or another. That's the issue.

So, how do you prevent yourself from making the same mistake?

Money and benefits are easy to compare, but environments? That's the mystery box. The environment is not just the energetic feel of the place, but the value system at play, the personality profile it supports, and the expectations that rule. Gun-shy, you ask yourself: *What should I be gauging about this company; its environment? How will I be able to tell if it's going to work for me or not?*

A quick gut check after an interview is nowhere near enough. Everyone's on their best behavior, and they'll tell you what they think you want to hear to further interfere with your internal radar system.

You need to ask the questions that can help you get at the environment component. Because you don't want to be hired only to discover, yet again, that the amazing job for which you interviewed does not exist.

You don't want to find, once again, that you've been "catfished."

Let Us Introduce You to Catfishing

If you've yet to watch Nev Schulman's riveting documentary, catfishing refers to purposefully presenting false or misleading information or creating a fake identity to fool another person. The practice may be used for financial gain or to compromise the victim somehow. (*The Tinder Swindler*, a Netflix true crime documentary, deals with yet another catfisher in the dating world.)

A catfisher hides all or some of their true identity in order to get someone on their line; the idea is that it won't be quite as easy to unhook and run. (If you're stuck in a relationship you hate, you know this statement to be true.)

Why do people catfish? You can chalk it up to insecurity—feeling bad about who they are in real life, wishing they could be more like some perceived ideal.

And catfishers don't just lurk in dating pools. You may sit across from one (or several) during the interview process. This type of catfisher will sell you a version of their company that doesn't exist to reel you in. They know what the average candidate is looking for. They know how to describe an environment, which they refer to as "culture," in an appealing way, because they know what sells. They've got the snapshot of the perceived ideal. They know the right bait to use.

Money and bennies out of the way, they'll tell you stuff like:

- We're one big happy family around here.
- We have so much fun being in the office.
- We're all about working hard and playing hard, too.

Like a catfisher on a dating site, they don't expect you to probe deeper or ask illuminating questions to help you decide on the fit because they know the right buzz words to quiet your brain.

A good salesperson, catfisher or not, is only focused on getting past your gut check, which is easy if you're not prepared to dig.

Here's The Problem

Maybe catfishing doesn't sound like a big deal. Maybe you've yet to be sold on an environment that can support your sense of meaning, purpose, and happiness, only to be met with something entirely different.

But a good catfisher will destroy any shred of optimism you possess.

You know the old square peg in a round hole analogy? You're the square peg that never manages to fit within the round hole no matter how hard you try. It's not anybody's fault, really; it's just that you're square, and they're round. We've all felt out of place at one time or another, so you get the gist.

It's even worse when you expect the opposite—when you expect to be surrounded by people similarly hard-wired. That's a problem, especially when you may be required to hang around and/or answer to them forty-plus hours a week.

It doesn't take long for unhappiness to set in.

Instead of bailing, you try to make it work for any number of reasons:

- You'll have to unwind the work relationship with all its sticky tentacles and head back into the market, which always sucks.
- Staying seems like the lesser of two evils, so you're committed.
- This is job two or three (or more)—you've already walked away from a book of business, a skillset that isn't always transferable, clout, seniority, benefits, or whatever. It's not like you want to do that again.
- You don't want to hear, "I told you so."

Next thing you know, twenty-some-odd years go by, and you're looking at a "failed marriage." Leaving at that point is even more expensive, painful, and tense. Those who bank on you are far less forgiving; your losses are much bigger.

You'll kick yourself for not leaving earlier, for not asking better questions before you committed, for taking a compelling statement at face value.

How do we know?

Early on, each of us got sold into a job that promised we'd be treated like entrepreneurs. That appealed to us because that's how we're wired.

Then we started the job.

Quickly we found ourselves stuffed into an Employer/Employee relationship that felt like we were trapped in a box. Not the large box of ethical standards, but a small one based on other people's procedures and principles.

"We're going to be your cop first, then your coach, and then your consultant." That's what our managers told us—not unlike the online date you committed to insisting you call them eight times a day after telling you they value independence. Neither of us wanted a cop. We didn't need a boss. We needed resources, support, coaching.

Both of us spent years playing defense so that we could get our own stuff done. The energy required was enormous—and there's only so much energy in a day.

In short, we were entrepreneurs who got micro-managed, and we didn't like it. We were young and naïve. We didn't know the questions to ask before we accepted a job to avoid landing in the wrong environment, the wrong culture. Which is why we want to give them to you.

If you want to enjoy going to work each day and being around others who think and operate as you do, you need to recognize catfishers who will ensure that you don't.

Out to Play You?

Leaders and their interview team catfish in business, not because they're evil, but because they lack the foundation required to create a fantastic culture. A culture is what produces a given environment. These leaders don't know who they are or how they want things to be, so they latch onto trending keywords or isolated ideas from some playbook on the internet and offer them up during interviews like juicy worms.

The owners of these companies are blowing money left and right, trying to figure out the whole culture thing. They know it's important to you—and they need you to grow their business. They need you coming in the door and staying put. They're highly motivated to see that happens, in fact.

We hang out with plenty of business owners who don't understand why their culture sucks; why their people leave in droves. They've thrown tacos at it, ax-throwing competitions, and countless rounds of golf because they think that should make the work environment feel fun. That should keep their people around. Except, random entertainment or questionable rewards cannot reduce the impact of much more significant issues. A ping-pong table in the lobby, for instance, will not make micro-managing an entrepreneur okay.

These owners don't realize their actions intersect the lives of the group in a thousand different ways; that it's their job to create energy and high morale so their people can overcome almost any obstacle and create opportunity out of nothing. Morale is all about the confidence, enthusiasm, and discipline of the group, especially when facing a dangerous or difficult time.

These business leaders have tried to boost morale through culture. Lord knows, they've tried. So they come to us for help because we're known for creating teams of diehard, loyal fans—for finding smart people who stick around for years on end, who rave about the environment to their friends.

We built a culture, not just any culture, but the kind of culture people call home. We figured out what it takes to create a culture that makes the right people want to stay. That turns them into raving fans.

By the way, we're going to refer to the work environment as "culture" from here, just to make things easier.

As it happens, only two types of company cultures exist: an intentional culture, which we'll explain as we move forward; and the unintentional or accidental variety, which often depends on catfishing to lure in candidates.

You'll find a culture in every work environment, regardless. A culture will spring up on its own in a vacuum. Whether you'll thrive in that culture or not is the question.

A Culture You Can Bank On

Our organization, our culture, which all our people brag about, is simply a product, a series of crafted experiences designed with a well-thought-out end in mind. It's planned, systematized, and executed with flawless consistency. It sounds kind of mechanical, but man, does it manufacture satisfaction and happiness. That's what you're after.

In an intentional culture which we've just described, the product is the client experience. (By "client," we mean you. By "experience," we mean your sense of the environment.)

Look, you're probably not interested in how we make culture, what's involved, but if we supply you with just enough detail, you'll be 100 percent savvier than most of the other candidates sitting in the interview chair. You'll be able to ask the right questions so you don't end up accepting a job based on chemistry and convenience, the way you might in the dating world. You can determine if the person across the table from you—and this could be an agent, acting on behalf of the company—has given enough thought to designing a consistent, targeted experience for you: if it's the right culture for you, first and foremost; if you're going to thrive; if they've got the infrastructure to deliver on their promises (or not), all the time. Basically, you can determine if you can trust these people to live up to their word.

Bear with us for the payoff, if you will.

Nothing in our organization happens by accident. Everything is intentional. Everything we do from a cultural perspective, every experience we create for our people—our clients—is intentional. We call them "monopoly experiences" because you can't get them anywhere else. If you love these experiences and you have a craving for them, we're the only game in town to offer them. Such unique experiences aren't random; they're, that's right, *intentional*. These experiences are designed to appeal to those who possess specific characteristics and values, making for cohesion. They're not for everybody, but they just may be for you. Walk through the door, and that sense of place you get has been designed in at least one hundred different ways.

We take this culture stuff so seriously that we score our efforts. Each well-thought-out experience has a line item associated with it—and it's evaluated, every quarter.

Laying the Groundwork

This leads us to an important point, one that's relevant to the conversation at hand. Knowing what you're after by way of culture before you start interviewing will put you on solid ground.

Do you, in fact, know what would make you happy? What kind of setting you'd want to work in? Could you describe it in detail?

Just as there are two types of cultures, intentional and accidental, there are two types of people in the world: those who know what they want and what makes them tick; and those who don't. Those who have identified what they value and those who haven't. Those who are aware of their key characteristics and those who have no clue.

If you're new to the work world, you may think you can't describe what you want, but that's not necessarily true. You've interacted with others—coaches, teachers, schoolmates—and know which dynamics work for you and which leave you cold and unmotivated. What kills your morale? You may think you don't know what you value or what makes you who you are, but you've developed preferences. You can differentiate yourself from others, which is a start.

Introduction

If you've been in the workplace more than a dozen years and still don't know how to characterize yourself, now would be a good time to start.

No matter your story, spend some time understanding who you are and what you want. You'll thank us later.

Even if you feel unclear now, the burden is on the company to overprove who they are, what they value, and what sets them apart, which will help you evaluate the fit. Your happiness, after all, is up to you to secure.

Buyer Beware

Catfishing exists, plain and simple. We can almost guarantee that you'll run into it during your job search. That's why we wrote this guidebook.

You, the candidate, need to be able to pull back the curtain and see what you're dealing with. You need the ability to make an educated decision, which is made up of two parts. First, is the environment you're about to subject yourself to appropriate for you? Second, is the described culture intentional so you can count on it being there?

If the answer is no to either question, chances are good that you're looking at a bait and switch ploy, something that looks awfully good at the outset but quickly fades, even before that first paycheck hits your account.

Remember, most catfishing is done by good people who lack a systematic and intentional approach to culture. They want you there to grow their business, not to abuse you. But the result is the same, regardless of intention. Many toxic cultures are born of good people who let entropy take over simply because it's easier.

Having good intentions and being intentional is not the same thing. Wanting a compelling culture that people rave about and producing it are different animals.

But how are you, the candidate, supposed to tell the difference? How do you know if the attractive wooer isn't selling you a predictable fantasy?

In the next few pages, we're going to provide you with five questions to ask while interviewing that will allow you to flush out a catfisher. This will enable you to be discerning and go beyond the gut check, so you don't get hooked. This process will turn you into the chooser instead of the innocent dupe.

We're going to show you:

- Why this question is important to you.
- What to look for in the answer.
- How we would answer the question.
- Your takeaway.

In other words, we're going to give you the tells so you don't wind up regretting your choice, and you can secure yourself a job with a culture where you can thrive.

This is a systematic approach to weighing an opportunity.

The pay is good. The hours work. The benefits add up. The culture is a fit. This is the formula for happiness.

Given what you will uncover, you won't be able to complain. If you're not feeling it, you'll have only yourself to blame six months in.

Based on how you weigh these components, this job opportunity either adds up or it doesn't. There's no mystery, just hard data.

One Big Happy Family

Question #1

"Explain, in detail, the target experience that you intend to deliver to your folks every single day."

When you show up on a first date with sweaty palms and high hopes, it's easy to forget to probe, particularly when you're staring back at someone polished and engaging. Boy, can you take a lot at face value when you're eager to shine.

But let's slow the action down. The dating site profile described a love of hiking. That's what made you reach out in the first place; what had your imagination running over time. But what does "hiking" mean in the first place? Would it occur to you to ask?

Nah, you're being silly.

Suppose your definition involves a 60-day, full-pack expedition up Mount Everest. In that case, the alternative of parking the car in the B lot and walking to the farthest entry at the mall isn't going to cut it. And that might be the definition given by the charming soul sipping a drink and nibbling on beer nuts across from you. In fact, that disparity will lead to some major disappointment once the honeymoon phase wears off.

Even if you think to ask in the heat of the moment, you might find the other person skirting the issue, offering up some meaningless phrase when pressed. "A day without hiking is a day without sunshine," they might say with a wave of the hand. Or "One man's hike is another man's stroll." None of that makes sense, but with a smile like that, does it matter?

That is often what happens during a job interview. Ask a question, and you may ignore the lack of satisfying detail in the answer, particularly if the interviewer throws in a few buzz words.

Why This Question is Important to You

Asking this question will no doubt surprise your interviewer.

First, you'll probably get a bunch of generalities which should ring the catfisher alarm.

Why?

The lack of satisfying detail at the interview table may signal a much deeper issue in the company culture. Culture, it's a thing. It's the feel of the place, the temperature of the room, the sense that you belong (or not).

It's an important clue if you want to be happy at work.

Remember, an intentional culture is simply a product, a series of crafted experiences designed with a well-thought-out end. It's planned, systematized, and executed with flawless consistency. There's nothing vague about it because the component details have been designed, then battened down.

We teach company culture to heads of industry, so we can break down the problem we encounter in most organizations: Few in a leadership position know what they want, let alone who they are.

They may know they need culture, that their culture isn't right, or that it sucks, but they have no real vision.

You can't deliver squat without a vision.

Squat is awfully hard to describe in detail to anyone paying attention.

This is where the meaningless phrases come in.

"I want our culture to be like one big family," they often say, which is always a sign that we have our work cut out for us. This should also be a sign for you. Let's call it likely reaction number two.

We all know families we don't want to go near. Family members who won't talk to one another, who steal from each other, who endlessly seek revenge and stab each other in the back. What does "one big family" mean? Because good and bad varieties of family exist.

When leaders say, "Hey, I want a great big family," they probably hope that such homespun imagery will attract people like you. These leaders don't know what their current people want, let alone an interviewing candidate, so "family" is the closest thing they have to a magnet. Who wouldn't want to drop their suitcase at the front door and come in, then curl up on the couch next to Mom?

Don't forget, this lack of clarity and overdependence on cliché is the reason for catfishing. *Sounds good; let's throw it out there, 'cause I've got nothing better.*

By the way, most leaders don't gain clarity on their vision because they think their mission statement covers it. They believe a candidate should be able to read the mission statement plastered on the conference room wall and appreciate the deal. But tell us, does that work? Have you ever appreciated, let alone been drawn in, by a mission statement? We know we haven't, and we've written plenty.

Sure, business leaders should understand their vision and what they're after. They should know exactly what accomplishing their mission entails—what it looks and sounds like. But you'd be surprised how often they don't. And that's bad. Bad for you.

It takes time to think through this stuff, to make a decision, and not every leader has the patience to work through the necessary process. So, you see, leaders aren't manipulative; they're just busy. Unfortunately, that doesn't mitigate the problem.

A great company culture starts with the end in mind. That's a big part of the vision. An intentional culture is designed to create an experience. That's the goal. An experience designed for the people it's meant to attract so they can thrive in it for years on end.

Here's the thing that most don't get (company heads included): a culture is the average of all experiences, not just isolated incidents, like regular Friday night get-togethers at the local sports bar or a Vegas trip for those who hit their quota.

The product isn't a random one-off, but a cumulative experience designed to appeal to a particular type of person.

What to Look for in the Answer

The person across the table from you should be able to paint you a clear picture, not offer you some half-baked generalities or clichés. They should be able to describe the product, the target result they intend to consistently deliver—not just once in a blue moon, but every single day.

If they can't give you details, they may have an accidental culture. If it sounds like anyone with a pulse would thrive in the place, you may be looking at a catfisher.

How We Would Answer the Question

To help you hear the difference between an intentional culture and an unintentional one, here's how we would answer this question:

We want a group of people who can be around each other all day, who respect each other, the team, and the resources; who work their asses off and challenge each other; who tell the truth even when it's hard. We want an environment of winners:

- People who don't accept mediocrity.
- People who take personal responsibility for the outcomes.
- People who create their own luck.

The Catfish Interview

That's what rocks our world because that's who we are.

We tailor the experiences we deliver to this kind of person, not just through the selection process, but every day after—from the time we further assess them, bring them into the company, and get them up to speed as a full community member.

Culture is the average of all the experiences we create.

We could give you a hundred different examples of a target experience we deliver on the regular, but let's focus on the feel we're going for, which equates to culture.

Our job is to build the biggest bag of carrots and offer them up to motivate our people. We don't keep track of advisors' comings and goings. We don't dictate how they spend their days. They'll have time enough to prove their worth in action, to make it clear that they deserve us to partner with them in their business. We chose to flip the whole boss-employee relationship thing on its head because, for people like us, the dynamic we'd once experienced left us cold. It goes against our shared value system. Work-life, the temperature of the office, the culture, and how it feels to be part of an organization, that there will make or break a person—and the business they're a part of.

No one comes to work for our company. Neither of us is going to be the boss. We bring the resources, the coaching, the education, and the leverage, and then we custom tailor it to each person's plan and where they want to go. Because no one does much of anything because we say they should, unless we're chasing them with a stick, which we have no interest in doing. If there's a reward out there that they can chase, a reward of their own choosing, they've got to run it down. Entrepreneurs will get up every day and go for it. They're the people who thrive in the environment we've created.

We threw away the regular playbook, sticks included, because the old way of doing things would never serve our end. We vowed to put everything we had into our people, into the relationships we had with them, and our shared experiences.

Our whole goal was to create an environment where people could make money and feel fulfilled at work instead of, *I gotta show up there at eight o'clock on Monday?! Please, please let me get through to Friday.* When you're fulfilled, when everyone else feels fulfilled too, it makes the experience 1,000 times better for all involved.

Your Takeaway

An organization may talk a good game; they may boast of a family-like atmosphere, and of Friday fun days. But without the details—how they deliver a targeted experience on the daily; who that targeted experience is designed for in the first place—you may well be looking at a pile of nothing.

If the person interviewing you for a position can't give you a sense of the place they've created, the feel they're after, buyer beware. If they can't paint a picture with a lot of details, you're likely dealing with a catfisher or, at the very least, someone with an unintentional culture.

If that's the case, you'll have no way of evaluating the fit, other than a gut check. Gut checks aren't particularly reliable. And a dazzling smile will only dazzle for so long.

Know Thy Self

Question #2

"What are the Core Values that people must possess to thrive in your organization's culture?"

It's easy to forget that we've got to have far more in common with those we spend our days with if we're going to be satisfied long-term.

Seriously, would you date someone who wants ten kids when you'd prefer to remain childless? Would you choose someone with whom to pursue a relationship if they expressed a desire to live with their parents and not move to the Bahamas, which is your dream? Would you be interested in someone who enjoys shopping all weekend when you can't remember the last time you entered a store that didn't sell groceries?

Laugh if you want, but plenty of people would and do.

It may only take one bad experience to learn this shared values lesson in the mate-picking world. But the need for congruence in the workplace seems to take longer for many of us to appreciate. It's even easier to commit to an organization comprised of people who lack similar experiences, feelings, hopes, and disappointments—all of which give rise to our core values—when you don't realize you have a choice. When you're being sold on a position by a smooth-talking catfisher.

For the sake of your happiness, let's sharpen that appreciation. Let's give you a better sense of control with targeted questions to ask, so you don't wind up amongst those who make your head hurt.

Why This Question is Important to You

The type of people you're surrounded by in the workplace—the behaviors you get to know, day after day—comes down to culture.

In a perfect world, company culture should be alluring to certain people who share much in common and want a similar experience. It should suit a particular personality, style, and take on the world. This culture should make certain people happy; others it should leave cold. That's just part of the design.

Often, what makes us happy is grounded in our core values; and by values, we mean key qualities that matter to you or a suitable mindset.

Who are you, what do you want, and why? How do you want the world to be?

Are you the one who wants to be surrounded by snapping sharks all day because you think that will make you feel energized? Do you enjoy swimming and biting others, too? If so, acknowledge your sharkiness—celebrate it even. Look for an environment suitable to you and your fellow hammerheads.

If that kind of behavior offends the hell out of you, who and what do you want instead?

If you don't know the answer to that yet, you're not alone. Business leaders often have a hard time getting at this stuff, too. It's why creating an intentional culture remains so elusive, and why they depend on catfishers to sell you into a veritable vacuum instead of a well-designed experience.

That being said, if you can't name your values, we suggest taking some time and digging into it, so you get clear before starting the interview process.

If you share common traits and values, you're bound to enjoy the same type of people.

What to Look for in the Answer

There's always a standard list of qualities necessary to hold down a full-time job that involves working with other people—hard-working, independent, friendly, conscientious. (Would you claim to be otherwise?) But what kind of responses might signal a potential issue?

The first red flag is a lack of specific actions attached to a stated value. In our industry, you hear the word "entrepreneurial" a lot. Yet it needs to be taken with a grain of salt unless the interviewer can back that up with a description of precisely what that means.

The Catfish Interview

It's all well and good to identify the values necessary to thrive in an organization, but if they can't be broken down into something demonstrable—something you can pick up on in your day-to-day interactions with others—then you're likely sniffing at catfish bait. (Remember, the day-to-days make up the culture, the feel of the place.)

The trick is to listen to the company's origin story: how it was formed; what makes it unique. Pay attention to more than what is said or what gets pulled into sharp focus. You can learn a lot about their actual values by what's left unsaid, or what remains ever so hazy. By the way, the fewer the details, the more sensitive your discernment should be.

Listen for the good, the bad, and the ugly, all of which led them to where they are now and formed their whole take on business and life. Listen to the "why" of the organization to see if the company's strategic goals are in line with yours. If you can relate, if you're in alignment, you may be on to something good.

Now, the person interviewing will assess your potential, using industry tools to that end; you can pretty much bank on that. They'll want to know how you did in your last job, what income you earned, the number of clients you had . . . but if they don't seem interested in your value system—if they fail to ask how a given value plays out in your life, why it matters to you—it's not a priority, for you or any other candidate. That's the second warning flag.

Once you get in, you'll be working with others who very likely don't share your coding. And that's bad on so many levels.

If the interviewer seems confused by the question or dismissive of it, that's a bad sign, too.

Hiring managers tend to get nervous when they hear the word "selective." You can be selective about your beer brand, or the kind of gas you put in your car, they think, but don't start down that path when it comes to new recruits. Many have hiring quotas they need to fill, or they can kiss their bonus goodbye. *If I'm turning someone around and showing him the door, where's the next candidate coming from?* That's the question they're silently asking. So if it seems like anything goes beyond satisfying industry requirements, beware.

On the flip side, if you're sitting across from a discriminating interviewer who cares about cultural fit, they're going to ask about several things in the interest of revealing who you truly are and what makes you tick:

- What's your unique story?
- Where do you come from?
- Who are you?
- What do you stand for?
- What obstacles have you overcome on your climb up the ladder?
- What dragons have you had to slay?
- How did your journey change you?
- What makes your struggle universal?
- What makes it unique to you?
- What's your big why?

We'll bang the drum again: you want the company you're interviewing with to be selective, particularly for your sake.

How We Would Answer the Question

Here's what a strong response sounds like based on clear core values, the ones we listed.

Our culture is 150% intentional. We are true to our target and are extremely focused on delivering on it every day.

Nothing in our organization happens by accident.

We have adopted a system called The Profit Culture Formula™, which systematizes every single interaction we have and measures it against our target outcome.

Anything we do is either on target, or not. Moving us to the line or pulling us away. If it's pulling us away, we either adjust it or get rid of it. We take this detailed approach to everything; every minute detail gets measured. Because the little things are often the big things.

The Profit Culture Formula™ also has helped us identify the people who will thrive in our organization. Folks that see the world through the same lens that we do. People that have the same inherent values.

We've identified four values that, if someone possess them, we can be sure he or she will thrive within our intentional culture.

These include:

1. Honorable: Leading with the truth even when it's hard
2. Own it: Accepting personal responsibility for one's destiny
3. Enterprising: Mindful entrepreneurship
4. Leveraged: Values resources and team environment

We also want to know that we can be in a room together and enjoy it. We've got to be able to see you and be excited to help you, and you've got to be able to see us and be excited to be part of this organization.

Much of our decision-making is born of experience. Yes, we know what kind of people will mesh with us, the environment and culture we wish to create, but we also have a history. We know the sorts of people who have thrived, survived, and bombed. We're on the lookout for the next addition who is a blast to work with and can totally blow it out of the water. We're looking and listening for those qualities.

Your Takeaway

The words "toxic environment" lend to the notion that there is an evildoer behind the scenes pulling the strings and making it so. Unfortunately, good people with good intentions often act unintentionally, selling the dream to someone who requires something else to find true happiness and motivation in their career. In the end, it results in the same toxic experience. And toxic simply means the experience or culture, whatever you want to call this thing you buy into, isn't designed for someone like you.

You want to share the same core values, pure and simple. You want to share similar energy, a similar level of what some people see as volatility, others as high energy and passion. You want to possess a similar ability to deal with stress. You want to share qualities that feed the culture around you. Most of all, you want to feel like you can thrive in the curated environment, that the culture was made for you. That you're hard-wired for it.

You are the company you keep. You want to choose your coworkers and managers as carefully as you choose your friends. Choose them more carefully, because it's safe to assume that many of them will become your friends.

The very same questions you should be asking yourself on a date—namely, is this person going to make me happy; am I going to make this person happy; are we going to be good for each other—are relevant to the interview process as well. Imagine the grief from which you could save yourself simply by spotting a core value match. Or not.

Good One Moment, Iffy The Next

Question #3

"What intentional systems do you have in place to assure that you deliver your target experience every day?"

Won over by someone who says all the right words, you buy into the dream. This is the start of a meaningful relationship; you can just feel it. Even your fingertips tingle. You value the same things! Your expectations are met, and then some. No sooner than you walk out the door, the text messages come pouring in. The promised outings to the vineyard or the ball game come at you fast and furious in the subsequent weeks. The fit is right because you can practically hear the click.

Then, suddenly, without warning, the object of your newfound affection gets busy. No more love notes. Your phone ices over; weeks go by without a sighting. Assurances are made that nothing's changed, but you can't help feeling abandoned. Oh, sure, you get tossed a crumb now and again, but that feeling is gone, the whole sense of the thing.

How could your initial perception have been so off?

Welcome, to dating hell—or an unintentional culture.

Why This Question is Important to You

The biggest difference between an intentional culture and its unintentional counterpart is experience consistency. An organizational leader has either put time, money, and energy into the consistency of delivery or not. And that inexplicable absence is what leaves you wondering where you went wrong.

Remember, from your perspective, culture is about buying into an expected experience so you can settle in and be happy at work for years to come.

Clearly, based on the first two questions you asked during the interview, the described target experience is right up your alley, and your value systems align. But (and this is a big but), if there's nothing in place to deliver on the promise, you'll find yourself cast adrift, concerned that you bought into a pack of lies.

It's one thing to buy into some description with zero underpinning if you're new to business. It's another thing entirely if you're uprooting yourself from a current position to find a better fit. If you're in the financial services industry, like us, you'll be transitioning clients for months on end, which feels like starting from scratch. In other words, you've got money and time riding on this bet.

Remember, most catfishing, at least in business, is done by good people with the best of intentions who lack a systematized and intentional approach to culture. The result is the same, however, regardless of intent.

At the risk of repeating ourselves, an intentional culture is a series of crafted experiences designed with a well-thought-out end in mind. It's planned, systematized, and executed with flawless consistency. It's something you can count on.

Whereas an unintentional culture may leave you feeling love-bombed one minute and confused the next. Motivated to kill it on a Monday, ready to call it quits on Friday. Surrounded by kindred spirits in May, flanked by annoying strangers in June. If culture is composed of experiences, if it is the average of all these separate experiences, the environment may feel completely wrong.

Now that you've identified a personality/energetic match, your job at this stage of the interview process is to determine if the company in question has an intentional culture or not. If it has a systematic approach to deliver on its promise, even when things get nutty. Because, be assured, they will.

So, does this company approach culture as a series of random events; or do they have a plan to create one well-thought-out experience after the other?

Without systems, things will fall through the cracks. Your sense of belonging and purpose will peter out. Your experience will be a crapshoot: good one moment, iffy the next.

What to Look for in the Answer

Many organizations go about the whole culture-building thing in a way that can only be described as "spray and pray." For them, doing the right thing is like using a shotgun versus a rifle. They tend to go off in every direction while assuming they're aiming at the right target (if they even have one). Instead of hitting the target experience dead on with the bullet, their efforts splatter all over the place. Sometimes they hit the rings by accident; most of the time they spray the wall. All in all, their efforts lack precision and have little cohesiveness, little flow.

This approach is nothing but a knee-jerk, emotional reaction. There's no systematic or business approach to it other than *I just kind of feel like it.*

In that, the first thing you're listening for is a sense of randomness. For example, in describing their targeted cultural experience, they'll tell you about:

- Breakfast Friday at the office with bagels and spreads.
- Karaoke contests at the local bar.
- The annual sales conference in Vegas for those who hit their quota.

Think about how these activities might make you feel: motivated; connected; annoyed? Then think about what sort of people they might appeal to. Is there a mismatch?

If you're hearing about a once-a-week or once-a-year event, how are they creating the day-to-day experience you need to be happy and productive? That's what you're after here.

Everything in the culture-building process must be aimed at creating, with precision, the exact product that will ultimately deliver on the target experience for a specific type of person—namely, you.

Then, it's all got to roll off the back of a machine.

When we talk about experiences rolling off the back of a machine, we're talking about the precise way an interview is conducted, how a candidate is onboarded into the company, right down to how you get your business cards. Every touchpoint, every interface you have with the staff, the environment, must be considered and optimized. Each of the associated experiences needs to be so special that you, the new hire, remain attracted to the organization for the course of your career. We teach this stuff to industry leaders and watch their eyes widen when we get into all the details well within their control. Details that delight all the freaking time.

This means the second thing you need to listen for (and maybe notice) is a reference to a system to deliver on a targeted experience, no matter what else is going on in the business.

Systems are required to deliver these experiences consistently. This is what you need to probe for. Without systems, you're likely to be subjected to random acts of annoyance or left wondering if you're still valued.

How We Would Answer the Question

This is what it sounds like if a company has a system in place—how we might answer this question:

We've got hard data that tells us if we're hitting the experience target or not. This data is all tracked in a system that we created out of necessity to deliver intentional results. It's called the Profit Culture Formulaä (PCF). The PCF manages all aspects of our execution. We can look at the associated scorecard and see if we're winning the culture game at any point in time. We can keep track of our current score. We can identify the places that need work to get the precise results we're after. [You can check out The PCF at theculturejunky.com/courses/]

This system gives us, as leaders, great control over the results we produce. We can focus on the targets we created for our company, those that position our organization the way we want them to, measure our efforts, and embrace reality.

This program allows cohesion, flow, and precision while eliminating the randomness factor.

The Profit Culture Formulaä scorecard helps us identify the gaps in our culture-building efforts and create plans to attack them. It allows us to pinpoint the holes and shows us where we've got to fix a few things by creating the right events. It shows us where we're failing to energize certain motivational types, and then how to measure the problem and the solution.

It has allowed us to identify the gap based on our value system, our culture, and the thing that we've aimed to create.

Everything we do is designed to motivate the kind of people who thrive in our culture. Knowing how to motivate different types of people makes us the cultural leaders in our industry.

If you really wanted to put us to the test, you'd ask us to pull out this scorecard and show you precisely what we mean. When we did, you'd be looking at a grid with hundreds of data points, each representing an experience designed with a particular type of person in mind.

Your Takeaway

If the interviewer doesn't know the answer to this fundamental question, they've got themselves a problem. And so do you. Because you may find yourself subject to some trendy, random nonsense. Or be left wanting so much more.

If, in response to this question, they ask, "What do you mean?" that's a sign that you may be looking at a catfisher.

If there doesn't seem to be a system to track the effectiveness of practices and events or consistently deliver on a targeted experience when life gets busy or a crisis arises, you may find yourself abandoned.

Yes, you may be a good fit for this company. Still, if they can't consistently deliver on the promised experience, you may as well be a mismatch, for all it's worth. And that there is the perfect setup for loneliness.

A Big Bag of Carrots

Question #4

"What are the top three motivators you accommodate for and give me some examples of each?"

It took us a while to figure out how motivators might show up in the dating world, particularly when dealing with a catfisher. But here's what cropped up.

You might yearn for a deep connection with a soul mate; for long walks along the beach holding hands, because that's how you're hardwired. But how easy would it be to succumb to a dazzling conversationalist in a killer outfit who talks about fun ways of making lots of money; who entertains you with tales of exotic trips and gaggles of influential friends; who can open a whole new world for you? You know, all those standard symbols of success—all that flashy stuff you spot on social media that lets you know you're looking at a real influencer.

Now throw in the added disadvantage of not knowing yourself well . . . of forgetting what you want in life has nothing to do with travel or cocktail parties.

There you go, all mesmerized, jumping into a convertible, zipping down the highway with someone who has wowed you, only to arrive in Miserableville a few weeks later. Fast forward a decade or two, and there you are, sharing your break-up story with strangers at some wedding reception.

Or you're sitting at your desk surrounded by people you don't particularly like, wondering how you can possibly make it through one more day.

Why This Question is Important to You

Motivation, if you're looking for a definition, is the force that draws you toward something. It can come from a desire or a curiosity deep within you or an external force urging you on, like fear. (Whereas a motivator is something that provides a reason or stimulus to do something.)

A culture is created around motivation, bringing in the right people who will thrive in the chosen environment; who will naturally want what a company's got; who will feel seen, heard, and rewarded. Culture is all about providing experiences that motivate the hell out of people who work there.

Interviewers usually want to know what motivates you. They'll ask about your "why"—why you're doing what you're doing. There are articles written that provide examples of model answers you can give that'll impress them. These articles explain that your answers should be honest; they should connect to the job by suggesting you'd be suited to the role. They also say that you should be able to back up your answers with examples from your studies, work experience, and/or extracurricular activities. They should relate to the skills and aptitudes required for the job you're going for.

What these articles may not tell you, however, is that you don't want to game it. Because you want to be part of an organization that can help you own the numbers tied to your actions and get where you want to be in, say, two years. They should be able to appreciate your desired destination. Your buy-in will be through the roof when they can make it easier for you to get there. If they can't, the chances of you being happy are next to nil.

Now, if you're supposed to be able to answer such questions with examples and details, so should your counterpart at the interview table.

This interviewer should be asking one thing about you: which motivator will this person respond to and which will be ignored? Which motivator will make this person hungry, and which will be deflating? In other words, the interviewer needs to zero in on your motivational style. (Just to keep things simple, we'll use the words motivator and motivational style interchangeably.)

Motivational styles vary from person to person and for different situations and topics. We draw on them all the time, especially when we try to learn something challenging. Individuals are driven by many motivators to one degree or another. One, however, will be primary, others secondary or tertiary.

Before you start asking your own questions about motivators and accommodations, it would help to know which motivational style(s) you possess.

If you have yet to determine yours, do the necessary work to better identify your primary motivator and the lesser ones. You may be surprised to discover that above all else, you value rewards, or power, or a sense of achievement, and not a fatter paycheck. You may be driven to perform by fear, not the prospect of recognition.

So, listen for your primary motivator. If an organization is interested in motivating those who are very different from you, you may find yourself a fish out of water. Unless you value inclusion above all else, that Friday Breakfast mentioned when you asked about the targeted cultural experience... well, that'll leave you cold.

What to Look for in the Answer

We're here to tell you that most leaders are trying to figure out what will make their people happy, motivated, and on fire, just aching to get to work. They tend to default to their primary motivator, thinking everybody else is hardwired the same way. They are most definitely not. Because there are many motivators—recognition, reward, inclusion, money, ego, to name a few—you can't assume everyone shares the same one, even though certain industries tend to attract one type over another.

Now, we'd like to throw in a little caveat. An organization can (and should) be composed of people of varying temperaments. Not everyone has to be a carbon copy of each other. Diversity in groups is a good thing. Diverse in terms of race, gender, religion, ethnic background—you name it. But where you don't want diversity is in the core traits. You want everyone to share those. That's where the power comes from. Diversity on the outside, matched with a uniformity of values that holds everyone together on the inside.

Leaders of powerful, engaging cultures—the intentional variety—understand that not everyone in the organization shares the same motivational style no matter how good the fit. They act on this awareness by creating experiences to keep their people motivated despite their predominant style. Their ability to do that well buys client loyalty for years, if not for life.

Motivating experiences stir the desire to go above and beyond the call of duty for some perceived reward. They inspire people to get out there and kill it and make serious strides in their careers. This helps everybody, on an individual level, be engaged in the culture so they'll stick around.

In an accidental culture, leaders are missing that key component. They don't get that everything needs to be directly connected to an individual's goal, to the desired destination, to inspire continued engagement.

In an accidental culture, there's little connection between a culture-building experience and the motivational style(s) they wish to influence. With any given event or process, there's little to no thought to which motivator they're attempting to satisfy—and with whom it will likely fail to get a response. The way they think, the experience (be it a contest, happy hour, or group outing) is all one thing.

How We Would Answer the Question

Our job is to build the biggest bag of carrots and offer them up. One carrot might motivate this kind of person. One carrot might motivate that kind. This carrot might motivate five people. All the carrots might motivate one person. But we've got to cast a wide net because we've got all different types of people, from a motivational standpoint, who fit in our culture. We have to make sure that we're doing things in each area consistently so that our net is wide enough to capture everybody. Systematically addressing all forms of motivation in a consistent manner drives tremendous results.

An experience is something that we regularly host or trigger to deliver a consistent targeted response, one tied to a given motivator (or five). We mean to deliver the experiences our people come to us for in a way that will make them want to stay and thrive. Notice we use the word experience instead of event. An event—a quarterly happy hour, for example—seems to be what people default to when addressing culture. It's that one thing they believe somehow checks the box.

We'll often create experiences like others do, through group outings and events, sporting activities, happy hours, and so on. And yet, every experience we create, uncommon or common, is about motivation, understanding who we're trying to influence, the motivational style(s) we're trying to key into, and why.

For instance, we do a summer educational conference halfway through the year. If an advisor qualifies, he can go and bring the whole family. What does an event like this capture in the room? What motivational styles respond to such a carrot? There's recognition. Then there's inclusion—I'm part of the cool club and all that stuff.

Now, during the second half of the year, we host a similar event, usually someplace warm and exotic, that's very easy to qualify for on an individual basis. Yet, we've thrown in a clincher. The individual doesn't go on this excursion unless the entire team meets the goal. In other words, you can't get there on your own.

Suddenly, we've triggered another layer of motivation, styles be damned. That individual—the one who values inclusion or recognition or reward—is all about motivating his buddy sitting next to him because he's made it and really wants to go.

We're very targeted. Here are a few more examples . . .

Sometime back, we wanted to increase family inclusion with our advisors so that everybody felt part of the team. We came up with the following solution: each year, every advisor's kid under the age of twelve receives a birthday card from leadership with a message and a two-dollar bill within. Believe me, that card and two-dollar bill go a long way in the creation of wow.

And while we'd done a good job supporting the recognition motivator, we wanted to increase inclusion and go even deeper with it. So last quarter, we came up with a way to draw in those closest to our advisors, the people who influenced them at home. It went as follows: the CEO replaces the traditional kudos note sent to an advisor, for a job well done, with a personalized short video. Since the videos are housed in text files, they can easily be shared with those at home.

What do we do for those motivated by rewards?

We've got a club recognition program that ticks the reward and inclusion motivator, as well as recognition. Each qualifier gets a branded golf shirt, like those that can be purchased through our marketing department, except there's a special patch on the arm signifying their club qualification and the year they achieved it. You'd be absolutely amazed how proud our folks are to display these shirts. They're positively on fire when they can collect them year after year.

What do we do for those motivated by ego?

Many of our advisors just like to win. That's what drives their performance. To that end, most of our quarterly incentives include an extra layer of fun or gamification. Gamification ensures that there's a winner.

For instance, we do a "summer madness" that mirrors the NCAA March Madness tournament. Everyone in the firm is randomly placed in brackets. Then, they square off against each other and score points following a specific set of rules. The winner gets their name engraved on the Traveling Trophy and receives a prize. So we also manage to tick off recognition, reward, and inclusion.

Your Takeaway

You want a path to engagement, the ability to control your own destiny with the opportunity to learn every day in a place where your efforts might just change the world. And engagement is all about motivation. You will do what needs to be done under the right influences. You will do more than is expected, which will lead to greater success and satisfaction. Motivation is the company's job. They must know how to keep you engaged in the game. They must create systematized events to keep you happy, to hit you where it counts.

Most cannot.

Bye-Bye, Warm and Fuzzies

Question #5

"How does your company adapt its culture in a crisis?"

Crisis has a way of opening your eyes to reality. There are countless articles that speak to this fact. For example, those claiming we could expect an increase in breakups during and after the COVID-19 pandemic; that divorce lawyers could count on being busier than ever. That's because a light suddenly got shined on our relationships. Once we slowed down, we could better see to whom we were married.

Working from home, illuminated the fact that the morning person you thought you'd wed is a bear until well into the afternoon; the neat freak has a penchant for leaving piles of files and dirty socks in every corner. What was it they said in their dating profile? *The early bird gets the worm? Who doesn't love matching storage containers?* Was that just to draw you in, or did you read it wrong?

Well, the same thing happens in the work world.

During the pandemic, the folks beating down the door for an interview suddenly realized who and what they were married to business-wise. It occurred to them that, given the chaos, now was the perfect time to pivot and make a change.

But a pandemic is just one example of a crisis that throws business completely into turmoil. Add a few years to your life, and you'll come across plenty more—a financial downturn, a natural disaster, a technical innovation that turns an industry into a dinosaur. Only one type of culture anticipates such and plans for continued stability when it hits. (Hint: it's not the unintentional variety.)

Why This Question is Important to You

The COVID-19 pandemic shut down the world. People lost their jobs right and left; the stock markets took a tumble; and folks had to figure out how to navigate a whole new world. That's about all the history any of us really need.

During the pandemic, most of our peers simply hit the pause button on their culture-building activities because they were in sheer reactive mode. "What we need to do," they said, "is make sure we've got money coming in." Granted, it was stressful for us all, particularly with infrastructure and many people to pay. Unlike us, the last thing they were thinking about was the need to create experiences.

Imagine how that played out for their people who were freaking out.

It's as though their company had suddenly abandoned them, had jerked from underneath them the warm-and-fuzzies that kept them attached to the raft.

No doubt that's one of the reasons we wound up talking to so many people. They were taking a good hard look at reality: not only had their lives been disrupted, but no one was responding to their needs.

We've all had to deal with a ton of uncertainty; it still lingers on the minds of everyone. It's shown us that everything can change on a dime. Managers and employees worldwide remain concerned about the future and are equally distracted and unproductive. But we've all got to stay focused. Leaders still have to keep their team engaged, even more so.

Engagement—feeling like you want to stay in a place that keeps you motivated—is all about culture. Culture is predicated on how a company consistently makes you feel. During times of change, the need for consistency goes way the hell up, not the other way around.

What happened to you during the pandemic? How stressed out were you? How did those you depended on keep you pushing forward in the face of uncertainty? Did they support you, or did you find yourself alone?

That's precisely why this question is so vital.

The pandemic may be over, but upheaval will crop up again, in one form or another.

What to Look for in the Answer

When it comes to crisis, you want an organization that is prepared for and knows how to navigate a shitstorm.

Unfortunately, many leaders believe culture can be set and forgotten. They don't get that they must remain in charge of creating, growing, and innovating it—that they must toy with it in an endless loop. That it must be adjusted and tweaked, even when times are hard.

If the person interviewing you has (or represents) an accidental culture, this question may cause confusion. In light of the pandemic, the doors are still open, and they're hiring. From their perspective, what more do you need to know?

Their answer may sound something like this: "What could we do with lockdowns besides jump on Zoom or communicate by Slack?" "*Who could expect more than a paycheck?*" In other words, they did next to nothing.

If, however, the organization has an intentional culture, the answer will somehow indicate that they do not abandon their people when times get hard—that they have systems in place to change and pivot as needed.

How We Would Answer the Question

Instead of falling apart like so many other companies did, business for us was booming.

When we recognized that we were dealing with a long-term issue, we gathered our people and addressed their concerns. We held a series of town hall Zoom meetings and came up with a proactive plan to deal with the new constraints.

Then, we got to work with the Profit Culture Formula ™ scorecard in hand, the very one we described earlier.

"Okay," we said, "let's go top to bottom on every impact point that we have, every single experience we create for our people, and let's adjust the ones we need to for this environment."

Twenty minutes later, we had a way to do everything we'd done before. We successfully pivoted.

So, yeah, like many other companies, we jumped on Zoom.

But we also kept up our regular rituals and added a few more. We kept our people growing and learning by delivering the latest educational topic of interest. We continued to share best practices, as we'd been doing for years because we know our team thrives when sharing with each other.

Team-building activities also gave employees a much-needed sense of security. These company-wide games—from opportunities for recognition, to the latest fun incentive—were essential for a couple of reasons. First, they supported a culture where people enjoy coming to work. Second, they helped team members build trust with each other.

We also encouraged friendly competition because many motivational styles thrive this way.

All of these activities worked to reinforce and continue to build our company culture. They helped form a camaraderie during difficult times. They pulled our team together in creative and interesting ways outside of customer projects.

How we specifically do any one thing isn't the point. It's the destination we're after, which is our target culture. The drive to that destination doesn't have to change at all. We may have to take a few detours to get around roadblocks, but after a few minor adjustments, our experiences remain intact, despite new constraints.

Now, if we didn't have our Profit Culture Formula ™ scorecard, we guarantee it would take a lot longer than twenty minutes to adjust. We guarantee you we would miss a bunch of stuff because it wouldn't have been front of mind. The experiences would change, and who knows how that would affect the relationship with our people. One experience affects the other and another and another. And let's not forget that culture is the average of all the experiences put together.

But with our systems in place, adjustments aren't a big deal. They allow us to keep consistent even if we have to switch everything up another dozen times.

Your Takeaway

Life happens. If it's not a pandemic, it's a market crash or an industry shakeup. Problems big and small will dominate; that's just how it goes. Without a clear target and systems to deliver a highly curated set of experiences designed to appeal to a particular group of people, culture—the net result of these experiences—will devolve. An accidental culture will turn chaotic. An intentional culture will remain the same entity you bought into, providing you with that sense of certainty and support when you need it most. If you smell a catfisher, it's only a matter of time before you wind up wishing you'd paid attention to the clues.

Conclusion

Why should you care if the company you're considering understands how to create culture; if the promised pay meets your expectations, if the math adds up, why put up a fuss? Why worry about the soft stuff?

Self-help gurus say that you should be able to bloom where you're planted. That you should be able to find happiness regardless of the environment or the circumstances you find yourself in. But that's not true. You'll bloom in the right kind of soil, and that optimal soil is different for everyone. If you're a violet, you'll wither in cactus soil.

Sure, you want to make good money, but you also want to be happy going to work, especially since you'll be spending most of your time there, with the erosion of work and personal time boundaries. You want to enjoy being there, around other people who feel the same; around those excited to come to work, those ready to make great connections and a respectable living. You want them to leap out of bed just as energetically on a Monday morning as they do on Saturday, just like you. You want them to laugh about something someone said in the office, the fun they had, the crazy income they see flowing their way because they're working their plan, just like you.

Think of it this way . . .

As a kid, you hung out with your buddies—you were in it together, through thick and thin. Half the joy was seeing how much everyone else enjoyed the shared experiences. And it was those experiences that glued you together for decades to come.

Nothing's changed now that you're an adult.

When you date, you look for a person who wants what you want—someone who thinks a perfect Sunday is one spent together, with a pancake breakfast, *The New York Times* spread across the bed, and an afternoon dip in the lake. Or (insert your version of heaven, here). Those shared experiences, based on personal preferences, provide richness, comfort, a sense of belonging, and well-being. They make you believe in golden wedding anniversaries and eternal love.

What you need in your personal life, you need in your business life, too.

As professionals, we sometimes forget that feeling. Instead, we surround ourselves with people we don't really like and do things we don't want to do because . . . why? *That's the way it must be; we can no longer afford to be idealistic.*

We need to remember that amazing things can happen when everyone is all in. When we're all in, life is good . . . life feels like something of our choosing.

Here's the takeaway message of this book: if you don't love coming to work every day, it will be your fault, even if you've

Conclusion

been catfished. It's up to you to shine a light on a company's culture. The truth will be revealed.

If you don't think you'll be happy there, you need to turn the job down and walk.

That means you need to focus on fit, and then the systems in place that ensure consistency of experience.

Determine the Fit

Like that gadget you buy on Amazon, a well-designed culture, an intentional culture, should be alluring to certain kinds of people—people who share much in common, who want the same experiences. The culture should make certain people happy; others, it should leave cold. And that's perfect.

But it means you need to break down what you're after in very real terms so you can figure out if you belong. That's what these questions were designed to help you do. Sure, you want the culture to be comfortable, but you also want to thrive. You want it to suit your personality, style, and take on the world.

Which begs the question . . .

The environment you're looking for, what's it like? Gather the details; get clear on the specifics and paint yourself a picture. Get serious. Have a target. Demand the same of those who interview you.

If you're going to be a happy camper at work, you need be around those who share similar qualities or values. So know thyself: who are you; what do you want most; what makes you tick? What do you value: learning; freedom; independence;

self-sufficiency; teamwork; sportsmanship; money; respect; attention?

This will help you better evaluate the answers to the questions and determine if the company in question is looking for a candidate like you—if you are the type of person they're trying to attract.

You may be tempted to go for it, without taking the time to ask the hard questions, to assess the answers. But don't think that misery won't impact you. It most definitely will.

In the absence of strategy, culture will just show up. This accidental culture isn't ideal or even close to what you want most of the time. If you're getting vague answers or canned responses to this set of questions, you're likely staring down the barrel of an accidental culture that won't even begin to deliver on what they promise, even if they'd like to. You could find yourself clocking in on a Monday morning, praying for Friday afternoon to arrive. Not one week, but for years on end.

Remember, a culture is created around motivation. The company's job is to generate feelings of purpose and personal growth for its people. *What keeps this particular person motivated?* What keeps you motivated. That's the question business leaders and recruiters should always be asking.

Motivated people make money for everyone involved. That's one of the reasons culture matters.

Leaders must be able to uncover the biggest driving force in the lives of their people so they can paint the vision that will pull them forward, particularly when things get tough. And things will get tough.

Check for Systems

Culture is not this touchy feely, feel-good thing; it's not taking some ideas off the internet and running with it (which is what way too many companies do). A culture needs to be treated like a widget, complete with appropriate raw materials, manufacturing processes, and supporting systems. It needs to be consistent and predictable, despite many moving parts.

To keep people motivated with the proper practices and events, a company needs systems. Systems are what allow for mindless execution, even in the middle of a global crisis.

Culture is not one event, practice, or experience: it's the average of them all. Culture is made up of the little things because little things are the big things, which is another reason systems matter. You know what happens when you've got a million little things to do. Something vital always falls off the plate. Throw in some major stressors, and a lot of things fall off the plate. That's when you, the person who bought into this job and culture, are left hungry and demoralized. That's when you start looking for a way out.

How can I differentiate the unintentional from the intentional? It's the foundation of the five questions. It fuels a deeper dive: *will these people be consistent, or are they set up to fail; does this company have an intentional or unintentional approach to culture; is this culture strong enough to endure a changing world, or will it cease trying to keep me going when they're consumed by other problems?*

Make the Right Decision

From an environmental, experiential, and cultural perspective, the five questions offered here should give you enough intel to make a confident decision on the appropriateness of any company with whom you interview. What you do with that intel is up to you. Just know that your future depends on it.

Much like the dating scene, on your job-hunting journey you're going to meet some incredible people, but many of them may not be suitable for you. If they can answer the questions, then by all means, listen to them. Take their stories in; ask for more details, an example, or further clarification. Keep asking; even if they're not right for you, they may be right for a friend. You can refer them. No harm, no foul. It's all about the match.

If they can't answer on the deliverability and the consistency factor, remember this:

Building culture is all the rage; most leaders say they want to improve their culture. They're trying. And a lot of them are succeeding. A lot of them are doing what it takes to build morale, particularly in stressful, risk-laden industries. They get that wanting something and doing what it takes to get it are two completely different things. Yet, other leaders have yet to figure this stuff out. They'd like to keep their promise to you, but haven't developed the vision or infrastructure to do so yet. Which is where catfishing comes in.

Now, you're savvy enough to pick up on that.

If we could wish you one thing, it would be this: that you slip out of the catfisher's net and land an outrageously good experience. So, here's to you—and being discerning enough to find yourself a long-term partner in your success.

Author Bios

Jon Corteen

Jon Corteen is a success coach, speaker, co-founder of The Culture Junky LLC, and CEO & Founder of THG Financial Strategies LLC. His belief is that a strong culture is the foundation for corporate growth and team member satisfaction led him to develop The Profit Culture Formula™.

Jon felt he was always on the losing side of the workweek battle: five days on, two blissful days off. Rather than waiting for retirement to enjoy all seven days, he founded THG and The Culture Junky, where he's since created and maintained the ideal company culture and now trains business leaders worldwide to do the same. In his opinion, we live too much of life at work to be unhappy there.

Jon graduated from Northern Illinois University with a degree in political science. He now lives in Long Grove, Illinois, with his wife, Gretchen, and children, Luke and Grace. He enjoys spending time with his family, focusing on fitness, and exploring the outdoors.

Jon Rotter

As co-founder and President of THG Financial Strategies, Jon Rotter leads the firm's new business and recruiting. Through the firm's unique culture and strategic differentiation, Jon is able to drive consistent growth and team engagement year after year.

He has continually attracted both new and experienced financial professionals who seek to engage with the systematic experiences of the firm. THG has received numerous awards from both industry organizations and individual companies, but its ultimate achievement lies in the loyalty of the people who call it home.

Jon graduated from the University of Wisconsin-Madison with a Bachelor of Arts degree in International Relations. He currently resides in Highland Park, Illinois, spending his free time with his wife, Lindsay, daughters, Logan and Remi, and son, Hunter. He is also involved in many different sporting activities, including basketball and golf.

Attention Leadership!

Get Your Free Bonus Material!!

Thank you for reading The Catfish Interview. This is where you discovered the 5 Questions your future candidates will be asking in their next interview, so they'll wind up happy at their next job. If you want to be ultra-prepared to answer them (and deliver a deeper and much more engaged experience afterwards):

Get your FREE Professional Power Interview Template

- Be prepared to answer 'The Catfish Interview' questions before you get asked!
- Differentiate and eliminate your competition!
- Hire more people!

The work world is changing exponentially and so are the demands of the workforce.

DON'T GET LEFT BEHIND!

Now's the time to attract and retain the perfect candidates, then to lead the pack.

Go to this website address NOW to access this key bonus content!

theculturejunky.com/bonus

Made in the USA
Middletown, DE
26 November 2022